Writing Performance Reviews

A Write It Well Guide

Revised 2014

How to write performance objectives, reviews, appraisals, and other performance documentation that is clear, descriptive, objective, and acceptable in today's workplace.

Write It Well

Published by Write It Well
Post Office Box 13098, Oakland, CA 94661
Phone: (510) 868-3322
www.writeitwell.com

Acknowledgements:

Author— Natasha Terk
Contributing author— Megan Willis
Original edition — 1994, Janis Fisher Chan and Diane Lutovich
Book design — Szymon Boniecki
Typography — John Richards
Editor — Paul Sterman

ISBN 13: 978-0-9824471-0-9

Fourth edition, November 2014

To order this book, visit www.writeitwell.com.

Advisors and contributors:

Many of the examples and exercises in this book were developed by contributing author Megan Willis, Senior Professional in Human Resources and Independent Human Resources Consultant.

The following Human Resources and Organizational Development Professionals reviewed this book in manuscript form:

Anna Bray, Training and Development, Appraisal Institute

Lisa Bretones, Global HR Design, McDonald's Corporation

Jonathan Hughes, Director and Business Litigator, Howard Rice Nemerovski Canady Falk & Rabkin, PC

Belva Jennings, Talent Development and Training, Unum

Bruce Lundgren, General Manager, HR Operations, Chevron

Alyson Margulies, Organizational Management and Development, PepsiCo

Craig Pampeyan, Director, Business Operations, Hewlett-Packard

Maxine Saunders, Training and Employee Development, Office of Human Resources, Department of Housing and Urban Development

Jill Silva, Senior Human Resources Director, Sybase, Inc.

Thanks also to Janis Fisher Chan, author and instructional designer; Lee Walker, design consultant; Richard Arthur; and Greg Terk.

To order this book, visit our website, writeitwell.com.

Our publications include the following books, e-books, and e-learning modules from the Write It Well Series on Business Writing:

Professional Writing Skills

Reports, Proposals, and Procedures

Land the Job: Writing Effective Resumes and Cover Letters

Develop and Deliver Effective Presentations

Writing Performance Reviews

Write It Well offers a variety of customized on-site and online training courses, including the following:

Effective Email

Professional Writing Skills

Writing Performance Reviews

Writing Resumes and Cover Letters

Technical Writing

Marketing and Social Media Writing

Management Communication Skills

Global Teamwork and Meeting Skills

Presentation Skills

Reports, Proposals, and Procedures

Train-the-trainer kits are also available to accompany these courses.

We offer coaching to improve individual professionals' writing and presenting skills. We also offer editorial, layout, and writing services to help individual authors and teams send out well-organized documents in language that's correct, clear, concise, and engaging.

For more information about any of our content or services,

- Visit writeitwell.com
- Email us at info@writeitwell.com
- Or give us a call at (510) 868-3322

CONTENTS

INTRODUCTION

WHY THIS BOOK

As a manager or supervisor, one of your most important jobs is to make sure your employees are doing the right work in the right way. That job includes helping employees improve their performance and, when it's appropriate, helping them achieve their career goals.

The first edition of this book was published in 1994 as *Writing Performance Documentation*, by Janis Fisher Chan and Diane Lutovich. While many things in the business world have changed in the past eighteen years, the importance of setting clear objectives and conducting thorough, thoughtful performance reviews has not changed.

In fact, well-written, clear, accurate, detailed performance reviews have become even more important as the employer-employee relationship in our society becomes more regulated and as more lawsuits are filed. Performance documentation improves the performance of employees and—if it follows the criteria described in this book—helps protect you and helps you manage legal risks.

> We are writing-skills experts, and we believe that everything you write is important. When we lead writing-skills workshops, we teach participants to use active, descriptive, specific, clutter-free language. It's not a coincidence that the same skills are important in both everyday writing and in performance documentation.
>
> Everything you learn or relearn in this workbook also applies to your everyday business writing. You can find ways to improve your general business-writing skills at the back of the book. Just look up the heading "Learning More About Communicating in Writing" on page 114.

In the past eighteen years, more companies have moved their performance-review systems online. These forms and ranking systems have become more complicated. But even though the performance management systems are stored and filed by computers, the feedback that's essential for performance improvement is generated by real people.

Your company's performance management process and system are unique. This book is not designed to teach you how to use your system. This book will help you understand why it's important to write performance objectives, reviews, appraisals, and other performance documentation that is clear, descriptive, objective, and acceptable in today's workplace. The book also offers you tips and tools to do just that.

PERFORMANCE MANAGEMENT AND EVALUATION

Clear communication is essential to effective performance management. A primary benefit of the performance planning and evaluation process is that it provides further opportunities to establish and maintain communication with your employees. For example, the process

- Helps you make sure that employees know exactly what's expected of them
- Lets employees know what they're doing well and what they need to improve
- Keeps you informed about what resources employees need to do their jobs
- Provides employees with opportunities to participate in decisions related to their jobs
- Enables employees to learn what actions they need to take to achieve their career goals
- Helps you avoid many employee performance problems and handle others before they become serious
- Provides crucial support for such Human Resources decisions as promotions, succession planning, salary increases, or disciplinary actions

For performance management to be effective, it should be ongoing—not something that happens once a year and is forgotten. No one should be surprised by what they find written in a performance document, as the issue should have been raised immediately after the inappropriate—or appropriate—behavior is observed.

Professional athletes rely heavily on feedback and use it to constantly improve their performance. Businesspeople should think of performance feedback in that same light.

The Role of Performance Documentation

There are lots of ways to collect performance feedback today. They include

- Internal and external client feedback (direct or through a survey)
- Peer interviews (direct or through a 360-degree process)
- Subordinate interviews (direct or through a 360-degree process)
- Self-review
- Results achieved against objectives
- Direct observation

Documentation includes everything you write down that concerns an employee's performance, including

- Performance objectives or standards that specify what an employee is expected to do to meet job responsibilities and how the person's performance will be assessed

- Survey results from 360-degree reviews or other survey methodologies

- Your notes—e-mails, memos, diaries, logs, notes to the file—that record examples of performance

- Comments and narratives that form part of formal performance evaluations or appraisals that support ratings, conclusions, recommendations, and/or actions

- Memos or letters to commend employees for exceptional performance

- Disciplinary memos or letters

Some documentation is temporary, such as notes you keep during a performance period and then discard after you complete the performance evaluation form. Most documentation, however, forms part of a permanent record that must be appropriately maintained and explains the reasons for performance decisions and actions.

It is essential that everything you write about a person's performance—whether it is intended to be temporary or permanent—be clear, accurate, and free from bias. Here are some reasons:

> **ONE NEGATIVE SCENARIO**
>
> Honesty and accuracy are important for job performance, and performance documentation can help you prove your side of a wrongful-termination lawsuit. If you fire an employee, the employee's performance evaluations must usually support (or, at least, not contradict) your reasons for firing them.

- A clear written record of discussions about performance issues can prevent misunderstandings.

- Clear documentation provides proof that employment decisions and actions were based on fair, objective, job-related criteria.

- What you write about a person's performance can become part of a legal proceeding. That can happen, for example, if an employee files a lawsuit to challenge a negative performance decision.

> **COMMON PROBLEMS WITH PERFORMANCE DOCUMENTATION**
>
> - Vague
> - Incomplete
> - Based on fallible assumptions

- Clearly written performance language can be essential to improving an employee's performance.

ABOUT THIS BOOK

We've designed *Writing Performance Reviews: A Write It Well Guide* to provide practical information, ideas, and strategies for writing more effective performance documentation. It doesn't matter whether your workplace is a huge corporation or a small business, a professional office or a nonprofit organization, an academic institution or a government agency. If you manage other people and need to evaluate their performance, the information in this book will help you write better documentation so that you and your staff can be more productive and get better results.

Program Objectives

When you complete this training program, you will be able to

- State the criteria for acceptable performance documentation and identify documentation that meets or fails to meet the criteria

- Write objectives and standards that meet the criteria

- Use clear, specific, objective terms to describe performance

- Support your ratings, conclusions, recommendations, and actions with descriptions and examples

A good performance evaluation takes time and saves time. By taking the time to write a well-researched and thoughtful performance evaluation, you'll spend less time throughout the year addressing gaps in expectations.

The following tips can help:

- Take notes on employee performance throughout the performance period, including specific examples as you see them happen. This will allow you to provide a clear, concise picture of the behavior.

- Ask the employee to provide a self-evaluation in advance of when you will deliver the performance evaluation. This request will allow you to see areas that you may not agree on and that you may need to emphasize in the written review.

- Write the review at least a week in advance of the day you plan to deliver it. Find a quiet place to work where you can reflect and not be interrupted. Review your writing before you present it to make sure it's clear and complete.

CHAPTER OVERVIEWS

Each of this book's five lessons includes explanations, examples, questions, and activities that are designed to help you write better performance documentation. At the back of the book, you'll find further tools and resources for learning.

Here's a quick look at what's in the book:

LESSON 1: Writing Performance Objectives and Standards

If performance objectives are specific, measurable, actionable, reasonable, and include a time frame, then employees know what behaviors and results will enable them to meet their job requirements. This lesson offers examples, activities, tips, and tools for writing performance objectives that encourage optimal performance.

LESSON 2: Criteria for Acceptable Performance Documentation

Performance reviews should describe behaviors and results. Keep yourself out of trouble by following some basic legal guidelines. This lesson offers opportunities to identify reviews that follow the criteria and reviews that do not.

LESSON 3: Using Descriptive Language

An evaluation of a person's performance must be based on observations of behavior and on the results of performance. This lesson highlights differences between reviews that feature observations and results and reviews that are based on impressions, opinions, or assumptions.

LESSON 4: Explaining and Supporting Evaluations and Decisions

Your evaluations and recommendations must be based on facts. This lesson provides strategies for making sure that you've backed up what you say in a review.

LESSON 5: Writing Specific, Complete Descriptions

A description is only useful if its details answer all the reader's questions. This lesson offers exercises and activities to make sure your review doesn't leave the reader confused or create any misunderstandings.

PROGRAM REVIEW

If you or members of your organization want to measure your learning or progress, then use the program review section as a test. The review section touches on the most important aspects of writing performance objectives and reviews and shows you where you need to focus your time and energy.

BEFORE YOU BEGIN

Keep the following points in mind as you read this book.

PERFORMANCE DOCUMENTATION IS WRITTEN COMMUNICATION.   Even though performance documentation has some unique characteristics, it's still writing, and the basics of clear writing are always the same. You'll learn a great deal in these pages about planning and writing a clear, concise performance review or appraisal. These techniques can also improve the clarity and concision of your general business writing.

USE THE BOOK THE WAY IT WORKS FOR YOU.   Each chapter addresses one topic. You might use it as a workbook—reading the chapters in order, scribbling in the margins, and using the Notes pages at the end of the book to record your own ideas. Or you might use the table of contents to jump right to the topic you find most interesting.

THINK ABOUT WHAT YOU'RE READING.   We've included questions to help you think about the material, and we've suggested ways to apply what you learn. Twenty-five years of experience working with adult learners helped us create job-relevant exercises and activities.

THIS BOOK IS NOT A GUIDE TO YOUR ORGANIZATION'S OR COMPANY'S PERFORMANCE MANAGEMENT PROCESS.   We haven't included detailed instructions for using your database, your rating system, or your review cycle. That information is unique to your organization, department, or enterprise. Instead, this book is designed to help you write performance objectives, reviews, appraisals, and other performance documentation that is clear, descriptive, objective, and acceptable in today's workplace.

THIS IS NOT A LEGAL MANUAL.   We haven't delved into the many legal issues that surround performance management. We're not lawyers, for one thing. For another, the specific legal advice appropriate to your situation may depend on your type of business or industry, where your business is located, which jurisdiction's laws apply, the size of the company, the number of employees, and dozens of other issues that could affect the legal requirements for your performance documentation. Here's the bottom line: this book does not offer any legal advice. If you have questions about your legal obligations, or the legal obligations of your employer or employees, then you should consult a lawyer.

YOU CAN USE THIS BOOK FOR TRAINING.   If you're a manager, Human Resources professional, trainer, or team leader, then you can distribute this book to managers who write performance documentation. You can also use the book as the material for a workshop (see our website, www. writeitwell.com, for information about our facilitator kits). Please contact Write It Well for information about how we'd use the book to deliver a workshop to your managers.

SCHEDULE TIME TO COMPLETE THE COURSE.   If you're working through the book on your own, be sure to schedule time to complete it. Depending on how quickly you work, each lesson will take between thirty and sixty minutes to complete. Turn off your e-mail, close your office door, reserve a conference room, or find a quiet space. Do whatever you need to do to focus on reading and completing the exercises and activities in the book.

COLLECT SAMPLES OF PERFORMANCE DOCUMENTATION.   This program will be even more effective if you can refer to a piece of performance documentation that you wrote. But if you have no documentation samples, you can use the ones on pages 106–112.

CAUTION!

Always remember that performance documentation can become a key part of a legal proceeding if a Human Resources decision is challenged. Consult your Human Resources representative if you're unsure what information to include, what a performance rating means, etc. And remember that keeping company records in the appropriate manner is a key responsibility in your job. Be sure that you're following your company's record-keeping policies.

1 WRITING PERFORMANCE OBJECTIVES AND STANDARDS

Performance objectives are also called *performance standards* and *performance plans*; they describe what an employee will do to meet specific job requirements. Clearly written objectives define expectations for the employee. They also provide a standard against which the person's performance can be compared.

Think About It: why do you need objectives?

Here are some tips for writing objectives:

- Focus on describing the results the employee should achieve rather than the activities the employee will perform.

- Do more than simply restate the job duties.

- Use the "who, what, when" approach. Clearly state what will be accomplished, who is going to accomplish it, and by when.

- Begin objectives with an action verb.

- Make sure objectives are SMART: specific, measurable, achievable, realistic, and time-bound.

Try It: write down one of your performance objectives here.

_____

_____

_____

_____

EXAMPLE

Jared's job description states that he is responsible for filling the book orders that come in on his shift.

This might be one of his objectives:

> Follow the steps in the "Fill Orders" procedure to fill each book order that comes in on your shift. All orders must be filled within two working days.

During the evaluation period, Jared's supervisor will observe his performance to see whether he meets this objective. If he fills the orders according to the procedure and within the specified time, his performance in this area will be considered satisfactory.

SMART: Criteria for Performance Objectives

To be useful, most performance objectives should meet the following SMART criteria:

1. Specific — Are they specific?
2. Measurable — Are they measurable?
3. Achievable — Are they achievable?
4. Realistic — Are they realistic, given the resources available?
5. Time-bound — Are they bound by a time frame?

Jared's objective meets the following criteria:

> **Tip:** Determining objectives is the same as setting clear expectations. If the objectives are clear, then the evaluation process will also be clear.

- *The performance is specific.* Jared must follow the "Fill Orders" procedure to fill book orders.

- *The performance is measurable.* It's possible to calculate the percentage of orders that are filled correctly and on time.

- *The performance is achievable.* Orders take an average of ten minutes to fill and, during an average six-hour shift, Jared receives 25 orders.

- *The performance is realistic.* Jared has all the materials he needs to fill the orders during the evaluation period.

- *The performance is time-bound.* Jared has two working days to fill the orders.

ACTIVITY: **Read the following objectives. Do any of them meet the criteria?**

Yes/no   Become familiar with the Department's Internet Usage Policy.

Yes/no   Learn the records management system.

Yes/no   Be able to balance client accounts.

Yes/no   Be able to prepare audit reports.

ANSWER:

Yes / **NO**   Become familiar with the Department's Internet Usage Policy.

Yes / **NO**   Learn the records management system.

Yes / **NO**   Be able to balance client accounts.

Yes / **NO**   Be able to prepare audit reports.

Here are examples of performance objectives that do and do not meet the SMART criteria:

Not This   Become familiar with the Department's Internet Usage Policy.

BUT THIS   Read the Department's Internet Usage Policy by May 17th. Be able to answer 10 out of 10 questions correctly when tested.

Not This   Learn the records management system.

BUT THIS   Attend a records management class and practice using the records management system with the assistance of an experienced coworker. Given a set of records two weeks after the class, be able to store them appropriately without assistance and with no more than three errors.

Not This   Be able to balance client accounts.

BUT THIS   With little or no supervision or coworker assistance, be able to balance client accounts within the time specified by your supervisor.

Not This   Be able to prepare audit reports.

BUT THIS   Prepare audit reports that meet the guidelines in the Audit Report Manual. Complete assigned reports without error by 4 p.m. every first and third Thursday.

Here's another example:

> Judy will need to show an improvement in her leadership behavior.

Written this way, Judy doesn't know if that means that she needs to buy a new suit, talk more in meetings, or work longer hours. It is important to describe the behavior that will support the objective.

> Sometimes it's especially difficult to quantify expectations or results. For example, you may have an employee who delivers great results but who seems to lack the leadership qualities that would allow her to move to the next level. However, in these situations it is even more important to provide specific examples.

Here's a way to rewrite that last statement:

> During the performance period, Judy will spend at least 30 minutes preparing for team meeting so that she can participate fully in the conversation. Her silence during the weekly calls has been perceived as apathy during her direct reports.

EXAMPLE:

> Bill will need to improve his attitude.

Written this way, Bill doesn't know if he needs to smile at people while he walks down the hall or if he needs to agree more often with his boss.

Here's one possible revision:

> In the next three months, Bill will need to find more constructive, positive ways to communicate. When Bill's peers offer suggestions at the weekly team meeting, Bill is the first to list all of the problems with the new idea, while rarely offering suggestions or additions to improve the idea. For example, Bill pointed out all the problems with the new software rollout without offering any alternatives or work-arounds. Bill can continue to address potential problems with new ideas, but he will also be expected to take time to research possible solutions to the problems he's inherited.

Try it

Which sentence in each pair best meets the criteria for a well-written **performance objective?**

1. _____
   a. Improve your e-mail responses to customers.
   b. Listen and respond to feedback about your customer e-mails, and rewrite them when you're asked to. During the performance period, attend at least one writing skills class.

2. _____
   a. Run more productive meetings.
   b. Develop and distribute an agenda at least three days before the meeting, and make sure that the meeting follows the agenda.

3. _____
   a. Review receipts each week and remind people on Thursdays as needed..
   b. Take more initiative.

4. _____
   a. Be more punctual.
   b. Unless an emergency prevents you from doing so, be at your station ready to work by 8:30 each morning, with no more than two exceptions each quarter.

5. _____
   a. Present a more professional image to the public by wearing standard business clothes as defined on page 57 of the Employee Handbook.
   b. Present a more professional image to the public.

6. _____
   a. Delegate more responsibility to team members.
   b. Tom should review the audit reports and provide guidance but not complete them; he should delegate the work to his team and step in only if there are serious problems.

The answers are on the next page.

1. _____   a. Improve your e-mail responses to customers.

   __X__   b. Listen and respond to feedback about your customer e-mails, and rewrite them when you're asked to. During the performance period, attend at least one writing skills class.

2. _____   a. Run more productive meetings.

   __X__   b. Develop and distribute an agenda at least three days before the meeting, and make sure that the meeting follows the agenda.

3. __X__   a. Tell Susie that you can't close the gas mileage account because you don't have everyone's miles. Review the data on Wednesday and send an e-mail to each person who hasn't turned in her or his forms, asking everyone to complete the forms by Friday.

   _____   b. Take more initiative.

4. _____   a. Be more punctual.

   __X__   b. Unless an emergency prevents you from doing so, be at your station ready to work by 8:30 each morning, with no more than two exceptions each quarter.

5. __X__   a. Present a more professional image to the public by wearing standard business clothes as defined on page 57 of the Employee Handbook.

   _____   b. Present a more professional image to the public.

6. _____   a. Delegate more responsibility to team members.

   __X__   b. Tom's team should be completing the audit reports, with Tom doing a final review only. Tom should be visiting audit markets only if there is a serious problem. In the next six months, Tom must stop completing the detail work on reports and must shift to a final review role. He should also limit his visits to markets, allowing his team to complete that work.

Here's a scenario.

Hal has been leading the Finance team for 10 years. At the beginning of the year, Hal's boss told him that to improve the team's work process performance, Hal needed to diversify the work experience and upgrade the talent on his 40-person staff. The department had experienced very little turnover; in fact, 30 of its employees had held the same position for more than 10 years.

During the past year, two of Hal's employees retired. Hal conducted an extensive search, interviewing many candidates: internal field employees, external candidates, and even candidates from outside the finance function. He hired one person from a field office and one person from outside the company.

Hal was very proud of these hires and expected to receive a strong performance review at the end of the year. However, when Hal received his performance review, he was surprised that his boss was disappointed with his progress in upgrading the talent of his team.

Why?

Hal's boss said that he was looking for a 10 percent change (instead of the 5 percent change that Hal achieved exclusively through attrition). He also wanted to see at least 10 percent of the department with field experience, and had hoped to see at least 5 percent of the department with experience outside the finance area.

Hal was very disappointed and told his boss that if he had known about these specific measurements, he would have acted differently.

HOW TO WRITE AN EFFECTIVE PERFORMANCE OBJECTIVE

The process of formulating an effective performance objective usually begins with a general statement that expresses what an employee is expected to *do*. Here are some examples:

- Learn something in order to meet a job requirement—e.g., "Learn how to change a tire on the service truck"

- Meet a specific job requirement—e.g., "Set up new client accounts"

- Improve specific job performance—e.g., "Improve your sales presentations"

- Demonstrate an ability to take on new responsibilities—e.g., "Be able to prepare budgets"

These general expectations, which sometimes come from the employee's job description, simply state the expected actions or behaviors. To expand them into useful performance objectives, you need to add certain details.

Depending on the situation, you must ask yourself some or all of these questions every time you want to turn a job expectation into a performance objective.

- What are the expected **actions** or **behaviors**—what exactly is the employee expected to do?
- How will an observer know that the employee has achieved the objective—what situation will exist?
- What standards is the employee expected to meet (how many, how well, how fast, etc.)?
- In what situation will the employee be expected to meet the objective—i.e., what resources will the employee be given?
- How long does the employee have to meet the objective?

Measuring the results is important. Here are examples of expectations that are impossible to measure, followed by the expectations written as objectives with measurements.

EXAMPLES

Expectation:	Reduce labor costs
Objective with measurement:	Labor line item reduction of 4 percent

Expectation:	Improve labor efficiency with high-speed pizza ovens in the restaurants
Objective with measurement:	Select, purchase, and install high-speed ovens in 100 percent of restaurants

Read these objectives and, using your imagination, apply a measurement to the objective:

Expectation:	Lower costs
Objective with measurement:	SWITCH TO A SUPPLIER w/ LOWER COSTS

Expectation:	Improve the expense reimbursement process
Objective with measurement:	DESIGN WITH AN MGCS TO MONITOR

Expectation:	Reduce the office supply bill
Objective with measurement:	

The answers are on the next page.

Here is one way you might have done it:

Objective: Lower costs

Measurement: Realize a product cost savings of $400 per month per restaurant

Objective: Improve the expense reimbursement process

Measurement: Reduce the payment cycle from ten to six days

Objective: Reduce the office supply bill

Measurement: By February, reduce the monthly office supply bill from $20,000 to $17,000

EXAMPLE

To write performance objectives, follow these four steps:
1. State the expectation
2. Ask questions
3. Answer the questions
4. Use the information from Step 3 to write a performance objective

Expectation

"A smooth rollout for the new program."

QUESTIONS	ANSWERS
What are the specific behaviors or actions?	• Test the time-tracking program for full accessibility and functionality
	• Develop an online manual and FAQ page that show employees where to enter their names; the names of the client projects they work on; the time spent on each project; and time spent on general administration, holiday and vacation time, doctors' appointments, etc.
	• Send out company-wide communications and launch the time-tracking system
What is the measurement?	By the end of next month, there should be at least 160 hours of data for each employee
What is the time frame?	By April 30th

PERFORMANCE OBJECTIVE

On April 30th, run a report from the time-tracking system that shows how much time each consultant spent on each client project, general administration, etc.

Practice

Four situations are described below. For each situation, follow the four steps listed on page 19. Then use your imagination to answer the questions and write the performance objective.

1. *Situation*: Sean has been working as a purchasing clerk in your department for almost a year. His job is to prepare purchase orders, keep track of purchases and supplies, and handle inquiries about orders. A review of Sean's purchase orders reveals that he makes an average of 10 errors for every 100 orders he prepared. You've noticed that he works very quickly and sometimes carries on conversations with coworkers while he prepares orders. He lost one customer order last month. His supervisor got a call from a frustrated customer who said that her e-mails to Sean were never returned.

   General Expectation: "Improve the quality of your work."

QUESTIONS	ANSWERS

PERFORMANCE OBJECTIVE

_____

_____

_____

_____

_____

Your answers may differ from the ones on the next page because you may have focused on different details. Make sure your objectives meet the SMART criteria described on page 10.

Here's one way you might answer the questions and write a performance objective for this situation:

> *Situation*: Sean has been working as a purchasing clerk in your department for almost a year. His job is to prepare purchase orders, keep track of purchases and supplies, and handle inquiries about orders. A review of Sean's purchase orders reveals that he makes an average of 10 errors for every 100 orders he prepared. You've noticed that he works very quickly and sometimes carries on conversations with coworkers while he prepares orders. He lost one customer order last month. His supervisor got a call from a frustrated customer who said that her e-mails to Sean were never returned.

> *General Expectation:* "Improve the quality of your work."

QUESTIONS	ANSWERS
What exactly is Sean expected to do?	Double-check all orders to eliminate all errors
How will an observer know that Sean has achieved the objective?	Beginning today, January 21, there will be fewer than five errors per month
What is the standard?	Enter all orders on time with no errors
What is the time frame?	Respond to all e-mails within 48 hours

PERFORMANCE OBJECTIVE

> Starting immediately, double-check all orders to eliminate errors, enter orders accurately into the system, and respond to all e-mails within 48 hours.

There's another situation on the next page.

2. *Situation*: John has recently been promoted to the new job of Safety Director at the construction firm. One of his new responsibilities will be to investigate accidents and write brief reports about what happened. The company expects that the number of accidents will be reduced as John raises awareness, informing people how accidents happen and how they can be prevented. He'll develop a safety awards program and increase the amount of safety training employees receive.

General Expectation: "Make job sites safe."

QUESTIONS	ANSWERS

PERFORMANCE OBJECTIVE:

_____

_____

_____

_____

_____

_____

Your answers may differ from the ones on the next page because you may have focused on different details. Make sure your objectives meet the SMART criteria described on page 10.

Here's one way you might answer the questions and write a performance objective for this situation:

> *Situation*: John has recently been promoted to the new job of Safety Director at the construction firm. One of his new responsibilities will be to investigate accidents and write brief reports about what happened. The company expects that the number of accidents will be reduced as John raises awareness, informing people how accidents happen and how they can be prevented. He'll develop a safety awards program and increase the amount of safety training employees receive.

> *General Expectation*: "Make job sites safe."

QUESTIONS	ANSWERS
What exactly is John expected to do?	Follow the report guidelines to write and distribute a report for all incidents within four working days
	See that John has developed, scheduled, and delivered monthly safety training for all on-site workers
	Develop and manage safety awards program
How will an observer know that John has achieved the objective?	Reduce job site accidents by 30 percent
What is the time frame?	Reduce job-site accidents by 30 percent by January 1st

PERFORMANCE OBJECTIVE

Reduce the number of job-site injuries by 30 percent by January 1st by distributing accident reports, hosting monthly training, and developing a safety awards program.

3. *Situation*: Melva has recently been promoted to a new job. One of her responsibilities will be to research problems and write brief reports. The reports must follow a specific format and meet specific guidelines. The format and guidelines are detailed in the "Report Writing Guidelines" section of the Operations Manual. An experienced co-worker, Alexis, is available to answer questions and review Melva's first efforts.

General Expectation: "Learn to write clear, concise problem reports."

QUESTIONS	ANSWERS

PERFORMANCE OBJECTIVE

_____

_____

_____

_____

_____

Your answers may differ from the ones on the next page because you may have focused on different details. Make sure your objectives meet the SMART criteria described on page 10.

Here is one way you might do it:

> *Situation*: Melva has recently been promoted to a new job. One of her responsibilities will be to research problems and write brief reports. The reports must follow a specific format and meet specific guidelines. The format and guidelines are detailed in the "Report Writing Guidelines" section of the Operations Manual. An experienced co-worker, Alexis, is available to answer questions and review Melva's first efforts.

> *General Expectation*: "Learn to write clear, concise problem reports."

QUESTIONS	ANSWERS
What exactly is Melva expected to do?	Learn to write clear, concise problem reports in the format specified in the Operations Manual
How will an observer know she has achieved the objective?	Review her reports
What is the standard?	Reports must meet the Operations Manual's "Report Writing Guidelines"
What resources will Melva be given?	The Operations Manual and one-to-one assistance from Alexis, as needed
What is the time frame?	Within six weeks (by November 2nd)

PERFORMANCE OBJECTIVE

> Within six weeks (by November 2nd), be able to write problem reports that meet the criteria specified in the Operations Manual, receiving assistance from Alexis as needed.

4. *Situation*: As a marketing assistant, Tanya spends most of her time helping develop proposals and marketing plans. But she is also responsible for planning and organizing off-site meetings—a task that Tanya has stated she dislikes and often leaves until the last minute. Something went wrong at each of the last three meetings she arranged, causing discomfort and confusion.

General Expectation: "Set up off-site meetings so they run more smoothly."

QUESTIONS	ANSWERS

PERFORMANCE OBJECTIVE

_____

_____

_____

_____

_____

_____

Your answers may differ from the ones on the next page because you may have focused on different details. Make sure your objectives meet the SMART criteria described on page 10.

Here are some examples for comparison:

Situation: As a marketing assistant, Tanya spends most of her time helping develop proposals and marketing plans. But she is also responsible for planning and organizing off-site meetings, a task that Tanya has stated she dislikes and often leaves until the last minute. Something went wrong at each of the last three meetings she arranged, causing discomfort and confusion.

General Expectation: "Set up off-site meetings so they run more smoothly."

QUESTIONS	ANSWERS
What is Tanya expected to do?	Reduce the number of problems in off-site meetings by reviewing arrangements with her manager two weeks ahead of time and confirming them with meeting facilities manager at least three days before the meeting
What situation will exist when Tanya has achieved the objective?	Meetings will be free of any problems that an objective observer would conclude could have been avoided by careful planning
What is the time frame?	Starting next week

PERFORMANCE OBJECTIVE

Starting next week, whenever you arrange a meeting, ensure that it will be as problem-free as possible by

- reviewing arrangements with your manager two weeks before the meeting
- confirming arrangements with the meeting site facilities manager at least three days beforehand

ASSIGNMENT

Follow these steps to write performance objectives for one or more of your employees.

1. Think of an employee who needs to improve performance.

2. Use the worksheets on the following pages to develop three objectives.

_____

_____

_____

_____

_____

_____

_____

_____

_____

OBJECTIVE #1

Employee _____

General Expectation _____

_____

_____

_____

QUESTIONS	ANSWERS

PERFORMANCE OBJECTIVE

_____

_____

_____

_____

_____

_____

_____

_____

_____

_____

_____

_____

OBJECTIVE #2

Employee _____

General Expectation _____

_____

_____

_____

QUESTIONS	ANSWERS

PERFORMANCE OBJECTIVE

_____

_____

_____

_____

_____

_____

_____

_____

_____

_____

There's space to write one more objective on the next page.

OBJECTIVE #3

Employee _____

General Expectation _____

_____

_____

_____

QUESTIONS	ANSWERS

PERFORMANCE OBJECTIVE

_____

_____

_____

_____

_____

_____

_____

_____

_____

_____

There's another activity on the next page.

Performance Objectives:
On Your Own

Take a look at some performance documentation you wrote.

If you don't have any samples of your own, or if your samples do not include performance objectives, develop a performance objective from Sample #4 on pages 111–12.

Copy one of the performance objectives you wrote or took from Sample #4:

_____

_____

_____

_____

Read that performance objective from the point of view of the employee. Then read it again from the point of view of a Human Resources representative who is reviewing this documentation.

List any questions either reader might have:

_____

_____

_____

_____

Use this space to revise the performance objective as needed:

_____

_____

_____

_____

You have now completed Lesson 1.

NOTES

NOTES

2 CRITERIA FOR ACCEPTABLE PERFORMANCE DOCUMENTATION

THINK ABOUT IT . . .

What criteria do you think performance documentation needs to meet?

Acceptable performance documentation includes enough information and uses specific, objective language. Here are the criteria for acceptable performance documentation:

- It describes behavior, performance, and results that the evaluator has observed

- It describes behavior, performance and results that others have observed

- It explains, illustrates, and supports the evaluator's conclusions about the employee's rating or ranking

- It documents agreements

- It tells employees clearly what they are doing well and what they need to improve

- It documents learning plans or other expectations for growth

- It documents expectations

DOCUMENTING PERFORMANCE CONVERSATIONS

Outside of the performance review period, managers often talk to employees about performance issues. It's important to document those conversations. Remember to write down the following details:

- The date of the conversation
- A complete description of the issue you discussed
- A note about any previous conversations
- A statement about what happens if the problem is not corrected
- A record of the employee's agreement to correct the problem

Every employee needs to have a combination of functional or technical skills and soft or core skills to complete their job effectively. **Functional skills** are *what* you do to complete a job (e.g., "finds the appropriate answer to customer questions"; "is able to reconcile financial statements with minimal errors"). **Soft skills** or core skills are *how* you do things to complete that job (e.g., "responds to customers in a friendly and professional manner"; "remains calm under pressure during monthly accounting close").

For an assessment, it can be helpful to separate the **"what you do"** and the **"how you do it"** of performance. These factors are also referred to as "behavior" and "results." Think of an employee you have worked with in the past who had excellent functional/technical skills but needed some improvement in the area of soft skills.

For example, imagine there is a customer service representative who always finds the right answers and solutions to customer problems. But while giving this information to the customer, he uses lots of slang, rolls his eyes, and sighs loudly when asked to repeat himself. As a manager, if you merely told this employee that he needed to work on improving customer service, he might try to find more complete answers to customer requests but continue his poor customer interaction patterns. However, if you separated the two aspects of performance, the information and feedback that you gave the employee would be more effective.

EXERCISE:

Look at some performance documentation that you have—either that you have written or that was written about you. Can you separate the technical skills from the soft skills? Rewrite one area of feedback clearly separating the two areas, ensuring that you write objective support for the technical skills and soft skills pertinent to the job.

> What performance information can you put in an e-mail? It's always best to discuss performance feedback in person and to clearly document the performance issue and conversation. E-mail can be used in these cases:
>
> 1. E-mail can summarize a prior performance conversation (although you should avoid e-mail when you raise an issue for the first time).
>
> 2. E-mail can help you work remotely or in a decentralized office situation. In those cases, be sure you describe observable behavior and avoid subjective terms.
>
> 3. When you cannot meet with the employee face to face, e-mail can help you deal with a time-sensitive or urgent issue (for example, one that could damage the business or jeopardize the outcome of a project). You can use e-mail in this situation, but you should follow it up with a phone call or face-to-face meeting when possible.

_____

_____

_____

_____

_____

Stay out of Trouble

Here's a process that will make your performance appraisal system work better and will also help keep you out of trouble:

- Avoid discriminatory or harassing language: it can lead to a lawsuit.

- Avoid jokes, racial slurs, and stereotypes.

- Avoid any comment about the person's race, gender, national origin, religion, age, or disability. These are characteristics that are protected by law.

If an employee mentions a physical or mental problem to you, consult with your Human Resources department or legal counsel.

> **AT-WILL STATUS**
>
> Most of the people who work for your company in the United States are called "at-will" employees, which means that they can be fired at any time for any reason that isn't illegal, and they can quit at any time for any reason. If you make promises or guarantees during a performance evaluation, you can jeopardize this at-will status. Avoid such comments as "This good work will guarantee your position here" or "You have a future here."

Try it.

Here are several sets of statements taken from performance documents. For each set, put a check mark next to the statement you think best meets the criteria on page 35.

_____ a. Cecile's clothing is inappropriate.
_____ b. Cecile often wears jeans and sandals or sneakers to work, although she has been told that the dress code prohibits such casual clothing for customer service staff.

_____ a. Daniel is at his desk ready to work by 8:30 every morning.
         b. Daniel is very reliable.

_____ a. Josh is very unprofessional in his dealings with clients.
_____ b. Three times during this performance period, I overheard Josh telling off-color jokes to clients.

If you checked (b) in the first and third sets and (a) in the second set, you are right.

Below is an excerpt from a performance document.

A. Read it and imagine that you are the employee, Melanie, who is being evaluated. When you're finished, list any questions you would ask the writer to make sure that you, the employee, would know exactly what you must do to improve your performance.

EXCERPT

Overall rating: Needs improvement

Melanie's work over the last six months has been generally good, but she needs to improve her performance in some areas. She likes her job and is popular with the other staff. At first she made too many errors in her figures, but she didn't mind being told about them and is doing better. She spends a lot of time on the computer surfing the Web and sending messages that are not work related to the rest of the staff. She is very good with customers and with computers. Looking at her desk, it is obvious that she has to work on her organizing skills.

List at least three questions you would ask the writer:

_____

_____

_____

_____

_____

_____

B. Now read the excerpt a second time, imagining that you are a Human Resources represen-tative who is reviewing the performance document because the employee disagrees with what's been said.

List questions you would ask the writer to make sure that you, the Human Resources rep-resentative, would know why the employee received the rating, "Needs improvement."

EXCERPT

Overall rating: Needs improvement

Melanie's work over the last six months has been generally good, but she needs to improve her performance in some areas. She likes her job and is popular with the other staff. At first she made too many errors in her figures, but she didn't mind being told about them and is doing better. She spends a lot of time on the computer surfing the Web and sending messages that are not work related to the rest of the staff. She is very good with customers and with computers. Looking at her desk, it is obvious that she has to work on her organiz-ing skills.

List at least three questions you would ask the writer:

_____

_____

_____

_____

_____

_____

_____

_____

Turn the page to check your answers.

Answers

A. If you were Melanie, you might have asked some of these questions:

- How do you know that I spend time Web surfing and sending e-mails that aren't work related?

- What is wrong with my organizing skills?

- What's wrong with the condition of my desk?

B. If you were a Human Resources representative, you might have asked some of these questions:

- In what specific ways does Melanie need to improve her performance?

- How do you know that Melanie "likes her job" and "is popular with the other staff"?

- What specific kinds of errors did Melanie make? How many errors did she make over what period of time?

- How do you know that Melanie "didn't mind being told about errors"?

- In what specific ways is Melanie "doing better"?

- How do you know that Melanie is Web surfing and sending e-mails that aren't work related?

- In what specific ways is Melanie "good with customers and with computers"?

- What is wrong with the condition of Melanie's desk?

- What, specifically, must Melanie do to improve her organizing skills?

On the next page is another version of the excerpt. Notice that the revision includes specific details that support the overall rating and also

- describes behavior and performance that the evaluator observed

- explains, illustrates, and supports the writer's conclusions

- tells Melanie clearly what she is doing well and what she needs to do to improve

Revision

Overall Rating: Needs improvement

Many areas of Melanie's work over the last six months have been satisfactory. She says that she likes her job, and in February she was selected as employee of the month by her coworkers. To achieve a Satisfactory rating, however, she needs to improve her performance in three areas: reduce the time spent on the computer doing non-work-related tasks; complete her balance sheets with more accuracy; and organize her work records in a manner consistent with the company records policy.

Strengths:

- Melanie is good with customers. She smiles and listens carefully when she helps them, and she takes the time to answer their questions completely. When she cannot answer a question, she politely asks the customer to wait while she finds someone who can help.

- Melanie has good computer skills. Using the tutorial and manual, she learned the fundamentals of Excel on her own in less than a week.

- Melanie responds well when she is corrected. When I showed her that she had made 32 errors in math on her balance sheet over a two-week period, she said she would be more careful and has since reduced her errors by 25 percent.

Areas That Need Improvement:

- Melanie spends too much time on the computer engaged in personal activities. At least twice a day, I have seen her looking at shopping sites or playing games on her computer. Three employees have indicated that at least once a day Melanie sends out non-work-related pictures, quotes, or videos to the rest of the staff. I have reminded her four or five times that this is an improper use of the computer during working hours, but within two days of each reminder I noticed that she was using her computer the same ways again.

Melanie has agreed to use her computer for work-related tasks and will stop sending non-work e-mails to the rest of the staff.

- Melanie still makes too many errors on her balance sheets. She has reduced errors from an average of 16 to slightly under 12 per week. She should make no more than five errors per week.

(Continued)

(Continued)

Melanie has agreed to double-check her figures.

- Melanie needs to improve her organizing skills. She sometimes loses track of paperwork and has difficulty completing tasks on time. I have noticed several times that Melanie spends extra time searching through large piles of papers on her desk. For example, she misplaced her benefits forms twice and had to request replacements.

- Although Melanie has been trained on the company records policy, four out of ten customer files she created last week did not follow the policy. The Sales Department returned the files to her so that she could fix them.

- For the past month, she has been almost a week behind the other staff in completing her customer response letters. The three times I have asked her to summarize the status of her tasks, she had difficulty remembering the status of each one—and twice she had forgotten about an important task.

Melanie has agreed to take the Time Management and Work Planning class that will be offered in October. Melanie will review the records policy again and ensure that the employee files she creates follow the company standard. In the meantime, she will complete a "TO DO" list every morning and review it with me.

You've completed Lesson 2.

NOTES

NOTES

3   USING DESCRIPTIVE LANGUAGE

THINK ABOUT IT . . .

What could happen if you use vague or subjective language in the performance reviews you write?

Evaluations should be based on fact—not impressions, assumptions, or opinions. Performance documentation should use objective, descriptive language to describe behavior and results.

> Try pretending you're a journalist—it can help you write better performance documentation. A journalist's job is to gather information through observation, interviews, and research, and then to write a detailed story that tells readers what happened. Journalists are trained to omit subjective comments and opinions.

Try it.

Which of these statements uses objective, descriptive language?

_____   a. The weather last Saturday was so bad I could hardly make myself get out of bed.

    b. Last Saturday, it rained for five hours straight and the temperature never rose above 42 degrees.

Sentence (b) is an observation. Sentence (a) describes how the writer felt; the characterization of the weather as "so bad" is the writer's opinion.

In fact, another person might have characterized the same day differently:

The rain last Saturday was wonderful—I spent the day curled up in bed with a novel.

Suppose your company announced that everyone could take a paid holiday on the next "nice" day—as long as everyone could agree on what a "nice" day would be.

- Joe says, "A nice day is damp and foggy. I love days like that because they remind me of my childhood in San Francisco."

- Terry says, "Oh, come on. A nice day is dry and warm with no clouds—perfect for a hike."

- Diana says, "You guys are crazy. A nice day is cool and windy. Just right for sailing."

You can see that because the word "nice" is an opinion, it's not very useful in that situation. Subjective words such as "nice" can cause serious problems with performance documentation because they are open to many interpretations.

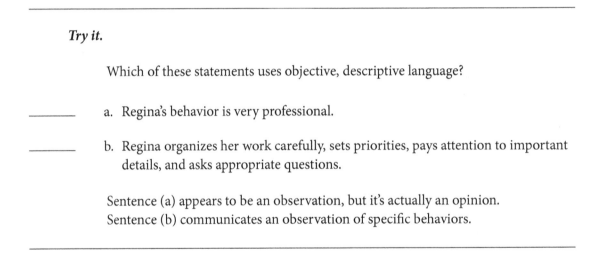

Try it.

Which of these statements uses objective, descriptive language?

_____   a. Regina's behavior is very professional.

_____   b. Regina organizes her work carefully, sets priorities, pays attention to important details, and asks appropriate questions.

Sentence (a) appears to be an observation, but it's actually an opinion.
Sentence (b) communicates an observation of specific behaviors.

Terms That Describe Performance

"Professional" is only one of many subjective terms people use when writing performance documentation. Others include

- appropriate
- adequate
- hard working

- sensitive
- poor attitude
- careless

Can you think of other subjective words or phrases you have seen in performance documentation—or that you have used yourself? Write them here:

_____	_____
_____	_____
_____	_____
_____	_____
_____	_____

The next page lists some of the terms you may have written.

Here are some commonly used subjective terms. Because they are actually opinions or assumptions, these terms require concrete explanations or examples if and when you use them in a performance document:

- professional
- strategic
- efficient
- friendly
- easygoing
- cooperative
- patient
- assertive
- likable
- responsible
- attentive
- punctual

- productive
- creative
- innovative
- candid
- accountable
- approachable
- respectful
- communicative
- unprofessional
- lazy
- disorganized
- argumentative

- defensive
- uncooperative
- impatient
- passive
- unpleasant
- irresponsible
- easily distracted
- sloppy
- time waster
- arrogant

Each of these terms communicates an **opinion**, an **assumption**, an **impression**, or a **conclusion**. They are each open to as many interpretations as the words "nice" or "beautiful." Some of these terms can be considered value statements. Some of them, such as "lazy" or "arrogant," can be inflammatory and should be avoided in performance documents.

Try it.

Which statement clearly describes performance without relying on subjective terms?

_____   a. Mary always waits for someone else to answer the telephone.

_____   b. Mary is lazy and doesn't like answering the telephone.

Sentence (b) is an assumption or an opinion about what Mary likes and doesn't like, and it uses a value statement.
Sentence (a) describes an observation of Mary's behavior.

> **TIP**
>
> Always use examples in performance documentation.

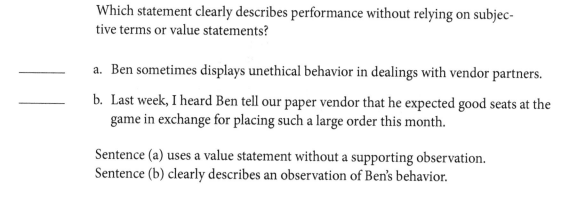

Which statement clearly describes performance without relying on subjective terms or value statements?

_____   a. Ben sometimes displays unethical behavior in dealings with vendor partners.

_____   b. Last week, I heard Ben tell our paper vendor that he expected good seats at the game in exchange for placing such a large order this month.

Sentence (a) uses a value statement without a supporting observation. Sentence (b) clearly describes an observation of Ben's behavior.

Use Objective Language

Instead of relying on subjective terms and vague statements that can be misunderstood and confusing to the employee, use **objective** language that describes **observations** of behavior, results, or both.

Clearly stated observations can help an employee improve performance by

- Providing a clear sense of what's needed and what isn't acceptable
- Helping employees prioritize their opportunities for improvement
- Ensuring that supervisors' goals align with employees' goals for themselves
- Helping employees determine where and how to seek the skills they need to improve their performance
- Ensuring that employees know what the skill looks like when it is achieved

Opinion   Susan wastes time.

OBSERVATION   Susan spends at least 30 minutes a day making personal calls.

Opinion   Martina is very dedicated to her job.

OBSERVATION   Martina came into the office three Saturdays in a row to complete an important project so the client would have it on time.

ACTIVITY: Underline the vague, incomplete, or biased statements in the following paragraph:

> Jane has been in the Marketing Department for six months. When she joined the department she did pretty well. She brought in some new ideas and worked really hard. Then when her ideas weren't immediately adopted she developed a bad attitude. Her behavior in client meetings is sometimes embarrassing. She clearly doesn't support the mission of the department and I don't think she believes in our products.

You might have underlined these words and phrases:

> Jane has been in the Marketing Department for six months. When she joined the department she <u>did pretty well</u>. She brought in some new ideas and <u>worked really hard</u>. Then when her ideas weren't immediately adopted she developed a <u>bad attitude</u>. Her <u>behavior in client meetings is sometimes embarrassing</u>. <u>She clearly doesn't support the mission of the department</u> and <u>I don't think she believes in our products</u>.

Try it.

Which statement in each pair is objective?

1. _____ a. When Jane finishes a job, she sits and waits for someone to tell her what to do next.

   _____ b. Jane has a poor attitude.

2. _____ a. Pete is a quick learner.

   _____ b. Pete learned to use the new database with only two days of training (the average is four training days).

   You should have selected (a) in the first pair and (b) in the second pair.

Practice

Put a check mark next to the objective statements that describe observations.

Objective?

_____   1. Lynn dresses very unprofessionally.

_____   2. With two exceptions, Dave was at his desk by 8:00 a.m. every morning during the past two months.

_____   3. I consider Justin one of our most reliable employees.

_____   4. Suzanne is very unhappy in this job.

_____   5. Sam is an extremely responsible, very well-organized, highly valued member of our team.

_____   6. Mary Lou completes all assignments on time, keeps accurate records, and contributes useful ideas.

_____   7. Although Martin says he has read the company's dress code, he often walks around the front office wearing a tattered sweater and baggy corduroy pants with patched knees.

_____   8. I heard Jason make offensive remarks (such as, "You're stupid") to coworkers at least five times during his probationary period.

_____   9. Nancy's letters are neat and error-free.

_____   10. Frannie is somewhat irresponsible.

_____   11. Pei has excellent judgment.

_____   12. Joelle takes the initiative by asking for new assignments as soon as she has completed a task.

Check your answers on the next page.

Answers

Objective?

_____ 1. Lynn dresses very unprofessionally.

__**X**__ 2. With two exceptions, Dave was at his desk by 8:00 a.m. every morning during the past two months.

_____ 3. I consider Justin one of our most reliable employees.

_____ 4. Suzanne is very unhappy in this job.

_____ 5. Sam is an extremely responsible, very well-organized, highly valued member of our team.

__**X**__ 6. Mary Lou completes all assignments on time, keeps accurate records, and contributes useful ideas.

__**X**__ 7. Although Martin says he has read the company's dress code, he often walks around the front office wearing a tattered sweater and baggy corduroy pants with patched knees.

__**X**__ 8. I heard Jason make offensive remarks (such as, "You're stupid") to coworkers at least five times during his probationary period.

__**X**__ 9. Nancy's letters are neat and error-free.

_____ 10. Frannie is somewhat irresponsible.

_____ 11. Pei has excellent judgment.

__**X**__ 12. Joelle takes the initiative by asking for new assignments as soon as she has completed a task.

Application

Read some performance documentation you've written. Circle any **subjective** terms you find—terms that express opinions, assumptions, or impressions rather than observations.

If you find any subjective terms, list them below. Then write an objective statement that clearly describes the person's performance.

If you don't have samples of your own, use Sample #1, #2, or #3 at the back of this book. Use your imagination to make up details if necessary.

EXAMPLE

SUBJECTIVE TERMS	OBJECTIVE TERMS
Shana is disorganized.	Shana's drawings did not include elevations or a materials list.

SUBJECTIVE TERMS	OBJECTIVE TERMS

SUBJECTIVE TERMS	OBJECTIVE TERMS

**In Lesson 4, you'll learn how to use objective descriptions
to support your evaluations and performance-related recommendations.**

NOTES

NOTES

4 EXPLAINING AND SUPPORTING EVALUATIONS AND DECISIONS

THINK ABOUT IT . . .

If you were a Human Resources Manager, what questions would you have about this statement?

> Jill is an asset to the department. She should be promoted to
> section leader as soon as possible.

By its very nature, an evaluation is an opinion or conclusion. But it is an opinion or conclusion that's based on fact. To use the performance management process to help employees improve their performance, your evaluation must be based upon a set of observable and measurable facts and you must communicate them clearly—both verbally and in writing.

When you evaluate an employee's performance, you must first consider behavior and results that you have observed or measured. It is the conclusions you draw from these facts that lead to specific decisions and actions.

Sometimes performance results are determined by what didn't happen. Here's an example:

> Alex and his team were responsible for updating our e-mail and calendaring system this year. One of the key metrics used to determine the success of this project on the user side was the number of calls to the Information Technology help desk during the three-month period following the rollout of the update. Historical data has shown that following a major update, the help desk experiences a 20 percent call increase related to the software involved in the update. Following this update, calls to the help desk related to e-mail and calendaring actually decreased by 10 percent. Alex's team's preparation and training in advance of the update clearly resulted in a lower incidence of help desk calls.

When you write a performance-related document, it must not only communicate your conclusions but include details that clearly support those conclusions.

Here's another example. Suppose you have come to the conclusion that your new technical support representative, Aaron, needs to improve his telephone skills. Which of the statements below clearly explains and supports that conclusion?

_____ a. Aaron isn't very good on the telephone. He can be hard to understand, and he isn't always as friendly as he should be. He doesn't seem to realize that people get annoyed when they are left on hold for so long.

_____ b. Aaron needs to improve his phone skills. He sometimes speaks too quickly and/ or too softly. At least seven times during a one-week period I noticed that he answered the telephone with "Yeah?" instead of "Technical Services," or said, "Hold on," instead of "May I put you on hold?" During the same period, two callers complained that they had been left on hold for several minutes, even though Aaron has been told twice that no caller is to be left on hold for more than one minute.

You probably chose statement (b). Statement (a) provides only unsupported conclusions and opinions. Statement (b) supports the conclusion with specific details that describe Aaron's behavior.

Here's another example. Which of the statements below clearly explains why the writer thinks that Benito would be a good supervisor?

_____ a. I recommend that Benito be considered for promotion to supervisor as soon as a position becomes available. He has consistently demonstrated his responsibility and accountability by completing every task on time and to the expected standard for his department. He sets forth clearly stated goals for each of his projects and ensures that every member of the team is aware of those goals. He has also shown an interest in working with others and ability for it. For example, he scheduled a quick weekly meeting with each member of the survey team so that he could make sure that everyone had the information they needed to conduct the interviews. If someone was behind or didn't have what they needed, he jumped in to help.

_____ b. Benito has helped us with a lot of problems in the department. When we were understaffed, he worked late. He puts in a lot of hours. I see him here all the time. He has stated that he feels he is ready for a more challenging position and would like the opportunity to become a supervisor.

_____ c. Benito should be considered for promotion to supervisor as soon as a position becomes available. He is an excellent employee, always reliable and responsible. He has been very helpful with the other staff, and everyone likes him. He's also very useful when there are problems. He'd like to be a supervisor, and he'd be a good one.

Statement (a) provides details that explain why the writer has concluded that Benito would be a good supervisor. Statements (b) and (c) provide only a series of opinions and assumptions.

INCLUDE DESCRIPTIONS

A description tells readers about

- The behavior you observed
- What the employee said
- What others say
- The results of work performed

Notice that without the descriptions, the following conclusions are no more than unsupported opinions:

Opinion   *This job may be too challenging for John.*

OBSERVATION   One of John's responsibilities is to make sure the high-speed printer runs smoothly. Twice in the last month, when John was asked to change the toner, Mark saw him banging the machine clips down with a stapler. When a co-worker asked what John was doing, he indicated that he didn't want to get his hands dirty. On the second occasion, he damaged the machine and the repair service had to be called.

Opinion   *Rishi's social skills make him a great service representative.*

OBSERVATION   At least six customers have said they like to be waited on by Rishi because he is always friendly and takes the time to answer their questions thoroughly.

Opinion   *Tom does not delegate work very well.*

OBSERVATION   Tom was promoted to leader of the audit department nine months ago. During that time, Tom has been working very hard to continue the exceptional work of the department. He is in the office 12 hours a day at least three days a week, personally completing many of the key audit reports. He has traveled to 12 of the 14 audit locations in the last three months. While Tom's work is excellent, he has not changed the way in which his department completes its work since he was promoted. As leader of the group, Tom would be more effective if he were delegating the majority of this work to his team, rather than completing it himself. Tom's team should be completing the audit reports, with Tom doing a final review only. Tom should be visiting audit markets only if a serious problem exists. Tom needs to review his work and the skills of his staff and then must more effectively delegate his work. In the next six months Tom needs to stop completing the detail work on reports and must shift to a final review role. He should also limit his visits to markets, allowing his team to complete that work.

Opinion   *Jennifer doesn't meet her goals.*

OBSERVATION   Jennifer has been working in the sales department for three years. During the first two years in the department, Jennifer came within 5 percent of meeting her targets. This year she missed her target by 25 percent. The targets were set in January and were shared with all members of the team. I met with Jennifer in January and she expressed confidence that she could meet the stated targets. During the year, Jennifer reduced her client visits by 50 percent. On three occasions, she sent outdated sales materials to clients. Jennifer also missed the annual internal-sales incentive meeting, stating, "I know all this stuff already."

Practice

Here are some more statements taken from performance documentation. In each pair, put an **X** in front of the statement that is a **description** rather than an opinion.

Description?

1. _____ a. Parker is a valued member of our group.

   _____ b. Parker comes prepared to meetings, listens carefully, and offers helpful suggestions.

2. _____ a. Henry is not a good team player.

   _____ b. All the sales executives agreed to reduce their '12 project budget by 5 percent, but Henry refused, saying that "his ship had already sailed."

3. _____ a. Three times during this performance period, an entire day's worth of entries was lost because Sol did not back up the database.

   _____ b. Sol is often careless and forgetful.

4. _____ a. Florence shows a great deal of initiative.

   _____ b. Florence took it upon herself to develop a new invoice tracking system for the company.

Check your answers on the next page.

Answers

Description?

1. _____   a. Parker is a valued member of our group.

   X   b. Parker comes prepared to meetings, listens carefully, and offers helpful suggestions.

2. _____   a. Henry is not a good team player.

   X   b. All the sales executives agreed to reduce their '12 project budget by 5 percent, but Henry refused, saying that "his ship had already sailed."

3. **X**   a. Three times during this performance period, an entire day's worth of entries was lost because Sol did not back up the database.

   _____   b. Sol is often careless and forgetful.

4. _____   a. Florence shows a great deal of initiative.

   X   b. Florence took it upon herself to develop a new invoice tracking system for the company.

Practice

The following statements are little more than conclusions or opinions. For each statement, use your imagination to add a **description** that supports, illustrates, or explains the situation.

The first one is already complete.

Opinion   *James does a good job and uses his time well.*

DESCRIPTION   James applies the best possible installation practices, relying on the NEC (National Electric Code) to be code compliant. He recommends needed services and sticks with the jobs until they are complete. For example, he recommended that we install exterior wall packs (lights) and additional external receptacles at the CCA-20 substation, and then he completed the job. He also installed a guard shack power pole at TQR and a more recent replacement of a power pole and service drop at KLP BIR area. During downtime, he restocks materials, cleans up the shop and warehouse, studies electrical drawings, organizes the lighting containers in our facilities yard, and keeps our work truck stocked and ready for work.

Opinion   *Dewitt is very efficient.*

DESCRIPTION   _____

_____

_____

_____

_____

_____

_____

_____

_____

Opinion   *Octavio disregards cube etiquette.*

DESCRIPTION   _____

_____

_____

_____

_____

_____

Opinion   *Michelle is not a good sport about her job.*

DESCRIPTION   _____

_____

_____

_____

_____

_____

Opinion   *Julia is a very strategic thinker.*

DESCRIPTION   _____

_____

_____

_____

_____

_____

The next page includes sample descriptions.

Answers

Here are some sample descriptions that would support and explain the opinions.

Your answers will differ if you used different details. Just be sure that what you wrote described observations, behavior, and results that can be seen, heard, measured, etc.

Opinion   *Dewitt is very efficient.*

DESCRIPTION   Dewitt plans his work so he is able to complete his first-priority tasks on time; then he uses the remaining time for second- and third-priority tasks.

Opinion   *Octavio disregards cube etiquette.*

DESCRIPTION   Octavio talks very loudly on the phone to both customers and friends, plays music from his computer, and sometimes sings. Even though his coworkers have asked him repeatedly to respect the collective work environment, he has not changed his behavior.

Opinion   *Michelle is not a good sport about her job.*

DESCRIPTION   When Michelle accepted the community event support position, she was told that it involved at least two evenings per month. For the past four months, however, her first response when asked to staff one of the events is that she is unavailable. She agrees only after being reminded repeatedly that staffing two events per month is part of her job responsibility.

Opinion   *Julia is a very strategic thinker.*

DESCRIPTION   Julia considers the impact of any proposed changes to the monthly audit reports before implementing them. Before she approves any changes, she ensures that both the creators and the end users of the report will benefit from and understand the changes. She clearly outlines the value to be gained from any change against the time and training it will take to implement it.

On Your Own

Read through some performance documentation you wrote. Look for an example of an unsupported conclusion or opinion and write it on the lines below. (If you can't find an example in your own writing, use Sample #1, #2, or #3 from the back of this book.)

_____

_____

_____

_____

_____

_____

_____

_____

_____

Now list the actual behavior you observed, the words you heard, and the results you measured that led you to that conclusion. (If you're using a sample from the back of this book, imagine what observations might have led to that conclusion.)

1. _____

2. _____

3. _____

4. _____

5. _____

On the next page, use the details you listed to write a **description** that supports, illustrates, or explains your conclusion.

Description

_____

_____

_____

_____

_____

_____

_____

_____

_____

_____

_____

_____

_____

_____

_____

_____

_____

_____

_____

_____

Make sure the descriptions you write clearly support your conclusions—especially if you are having difficulty clearly stating your observations. It's often helpful to have someone—a peer or Human Resources representative—review your performance documentation. See whether this person has questions about any of your statements.

You've completed Lesson 4.

NOTES

NOTES

5   WRITING SPECIFIC, COMPLETE DESCRIPTIONS

A description is useful only if its details are specific and complete. Which of these descriptions provides the most useful information?

_____ a. The tennis match between two well-known players lasted a long time. Two sets had to be decided by tiebreakers. The final score was very close.

_____ b. The tennis match between Venus and Serena Williams lasted for three and a half hours. The first and third sets had to be decided by tiebreakers. Serena finally won, 7–6, 4–6, 7–6.

You can easily see that description (b) uses more specific details and is more complete. It answers key questions: How long was "a long time"? Which "two sets" were decided by tiebreakers? Who are the "well-known" players? What was the "very close" final score?

A description that includes complete, specific details answers these kinds of questions:

- How long?
- How many?
- Where?
- How often?
- When?
- Who?

> **RE-READ YOUR DOCUMENT.**
>
> Ask yourself if there are any important details missing, anything that is personal and not fact-based, or anything that could be misinterpreted.

What are the questions you would ask about the following description?

Sue frequently takes long breaks. She is also sometimes late when she returns to the office from lunch.

_____

_____

_____

You might ask,

- How often does Sue take long breaks?

- How long are the breaks?

- How often is she late after lunch?

- When she is late, how late is she?

You might also ask how the evaluator knew that Sue took long breaks and was often late.

Here's a more complete, specific description:

> Of the 15 breaks observed in the past three months, Sue has returned ten to fifteen minutes late on six occasions and more than fifteen minutes late on three occasions. I also noted that on nine occasions she was fifteen to thirty minutes late returning from lunch.

> **TIP**
>
> Establish a filing system that both managers and employees will use to track accomplishments, making it less difficult to pull together the information at the end of the year.

Here are some more examples of vague, incomplete descriptions. Each example is followed by a revision that includes complete, specific details.

Incomplete	James does not always follow safety regulations.
COMPLETE	During each of the last five fire drills scheduled during James's night shifts, coworkers report that James kept right on working.
Incomplete	Howard has an excellent ability to meet deadlines.
COMPLETE	Eleven of the twelve reports Howard was assigned during the last six months were turned in early or on time.
Incomplete	Elly does not prioritize her work effectively.
COMPLETE	On three occasions in the past month, Elly has completed all of her transcribing work before completing the department schedules, despite being told on each occasion that the department schedules must be her first priority.

Try it.

Here are some descriptions of employee performance. Put an **X** in front of the descriptions that are **incomplete, vague,** or both.

Incomplete and/or Vague?

_____   1. Joe rarely balances his books.

_____   2. During a five-month period, we received four letters from customers commenting on how much Alicia helped them.

_____   3. Often, Jim fails to sign out when he leaves to make a delivery.

_____   4. I overheard Cynthia tell a customer that the customer's sister had overdrawn her checking account.

_____   5. Lorenzo closes more sales than any other salesperson on our staff.

Check your answers on the next page.

ANSWERS

The check marks indicate descriptions that lack important details.

Incomplete and/or Vague?

__X__   1. Joe rarely balances his books.

_____   2. During a five-month period, we received four letters from customers commenting on how much Alicia helped them.

__X__   3. Often, Jim fails to sign out when he leaves to make a delivery.

_____   4. I overheard Cynthia tell a customer that the customer's sister had overdrawn her checking account.

__X__   5. Lorenzo closes more sales than any other salesperson on our staff.

Now look at the incomplete descriptions again. This time, list the questions you would ask about each description:

___**X**___   Joe rarely balances his books.

Questions   _____

_____

_____

_____

_____

___**X**___   Often, Jim fails to sign out when he leaves to make a delivery.

Questions   _____

_____

_____

_____

_____

___**X**___   Lorenzo closes more sales than any other salesperson on our staff.

Questions   _____

_____

_____

_____

_____

Turn the page to see examples of the kinds of questions you might have listed.

Here are some examples of questions you might have listed:

___**X**___   Joe rarely balances his books.

How often does he fail to balance his books?

How often is he expected to balance them?

How do you (the evaluator) know he fails to balance them?

___**X**___   Often, Jim fails to sign out when he leaves to make a delivery.

How often does Joe fail to sign out?

Has he been reminded?

___**X**___   Lorenzo closes more sales than any other salesperson on our staff.

How many more sales, or what percentage more sales, does Lorenzo make?

For what period of time has Lorenzo made more sales?

Does "more" mean the number of sales or the dollar amount?

Practice

Below and on the next page are several incomplete, vague descriptions.

- List the questions you would ask about these descriptions.
- Use your imagination to answer the questions so you can revise the descriptions.

1. *For some time now, Patrick has been the most productive proofreader in our department.*

Questions

REVISION

2. *With people all over the globe, Meade did a great job managing the work environment.*

Questions   _____

_____

_____

_____

_____

_____

REVISION   _____

_____

_____

_____

_____

_____

_____

_____

_____

_____

_____

The practice continues on the next page.

3.   *I have noticed that Maria is very good with her staff.*

Questions   _____

_____

_____

_____

_____

_____

REVISION   _____

_____

_____

_____

_____

_____

_____

_____

_____

_____

_____

Answers

Your answers will differ. But you should have asked the key questions and provided details to answer them in your revisions.

1. *For some time now, Patrick has been the most productive proofreader in our department.*

Questions

- How long is "some time now"?

- How is productivity measured?

- Does he read more copy? Does he read it faster?

- Does he catch more errors?

- What does "most productive" mean?

REVISION

For the past six months, Patrick has completed twice as many projects as anyone else on the proofreading staff, and each one of them has been error-free.

2.   *With people all over the globe, Meade did a great job managing the work environment.*

Questions

- What does "all over the globe" mean?

- What does he manage?

- What's challenging about the work environment?

- What did he do well?

REVISION

Meade manages 12 people in nine countries. By using technology (weekly video conferences, monthly Web-based meetings, and quarterly workshops), he sent extremely clear direct reports from India about the business unit's goals and challenges.

3.   *I have noticed that Maria is very good with her staff.*

Questions

- What does Maria do that shows she is "very good with her staff"?

- What does the staff say about her?

REVISION

During this performance period, Maria has met at least once a week with each of the three employees she supervises to discuss progress, answer questions, and calibrate the distribution of the team workload.

Turn the page for examples of other questions to ask.

Other Questions

In addition to such questions as "how many" and "how often," useful descriptions might need to answer some other questions, such as

- How was the information obtained—observation? measurement? conversation? survey? interviews?

- What is the standard with which the performance is being compared?

- Does the employee know what he or she is expected to do?

- Does the employee have the skills and resources needed to achieve satisfactory performance?

- If the performance is less than satisfactory, has the employee been reminded that it needs to be improved?

- Why is this performance important?

A well-written performance review should contain the following information and sections:

- Performance expectations or objectives, established at the beginning of the period

- A listing of accomplishments or results achieved during the performance period

- Narrative descriptions of how performance results were achieved, including specific examples of strengths as well as areas where improvement is necessary

- A rating of the performance based upon your company's current guidelines

EXAMPLE

Original   *Darya routinely misses department meetings.*

QUESTIONS	ANSWERS
What does "routinely" mean?	*She missed 9 out of 20 meetings this quarter*
How was this information obtained?	*Direct observations and review of attendance records*
Is there an established standard of performance regarding attendance of meetings? If so, what is the standard?	*All staff members are expected to attend all meetings unless they are ill, away from the office on business, or on vacation*
Does Darya know she is expected to attend?	*The job description and last performance evaluation clearly state that she is expected to attend all meetings*
Does Darya lack any skills or resources she would need to improve this performance?	*She says she doesn't have time to attend meetings and that when she is busy, she forgets about them*
Has Darya been reminded that she is expected to attend? If so, how many times?	*She has been told four times during the past quarter*
Why is it important that Darya attend?	*She needs information from others to do her job*
	Others need information, ideas, and suggestions from her

REVISION

Attendance records indicate that Darya missed 9 out of 20 department meetings this quarter, even though all staff are expected to attend all meetings (unless they are ill, away from the office on business, or on vacation). Her job description and her last written performance evaluation, which occurred three months ago, state this expectation.

Darya says that she misses meetings because she doesn't have the time; when she is busy, she forgets about meetings. I discussed this matter with her four times during the quarter. I reminded her that the meetings are important because they provide her with information she needs to do her job and give other staff a chance to get her ideas and suggestions.

Try it.

Below is a vague, incomplete description of performance.

- List the questions you would ask, and use your imagination to answer them.
- Revise the description to answer all the questions that are relevant to this situation.

Original   *Berwin sometimes fails to provide sufficient orientation for new employees in his department.*

QUESTIONS	ANSWERS

REVISION

_____

_____

_____

_____

_____

_____

_____

_____

_____

_____

_____

_____

_____

Turn the page to check your answers.

Answer

Your answers will differ, but you should have asked the key questions below, and your answers should have provided complete and specific descriptions. Here are some questions you might have asked and examples of answers you might have listed.

Original   *Berwin sometimes fails to provide sufficient orientation for new employees in his department.*

QUESTIONS	ANSWERS
What does "sometimes" mean?	• Three out of seven new employees did not receive sufficient orientation during the last quarter
What would "sufficient orientation" be?	• A review of the New Employee Manual and an opportunity to ask questions
	• A description of the nature of our business and the department's role in achieving company objectives
	• An introduction to the other staff members
	• A tour of the facility
In what ways is the orientation not sufficient?	• Two employees were only handed the manual and told to read it, with no opportunity to ask questions
	• None of the three employees was given a description of the business
	• One of the employees was not introduced to the other staff members
	• None of the employees was given a tour
How was this information obtained?	• Routine interviews of new employees
Does Berwin know what is expected?	• It is in his job description
	• The steps were reviewed with him when he became a manager a year ago and again six months ago

Here's a possible revision of the original description.

REVISION

Routine interviews of the seven new employees Berwin hired during the last quarter reveal that three of them failed to receive sufficient orientation.

Berwin is expected to review the New Employee Manual with new staff and give them a chance to ask questions. Yet two of the three employees were only handed the manual and told to read it, with no opportunity to ask questions.

Berwin is supposed to describe the nature of our business and the department's role in achieving company objectives; none of the three employees was given this description.

Berwin is supposed to introduce new employees to other department staff and give them a tour of the facility; one of the three employees was not introduced to other staff members and none of the three was given a tour.

Berwin's job description clearly states the steps he is expected to take to provide orientation. I reviewed those steps with him when he took the manager's position a year ago and again six months ago during our mid-year discussion.

There's another practice on the next page.

Practice

Below is a paragraph taken from a performance evaluation.

- List the key questions you would ask if you were the employee or a Human Resources representative reviewing the description, and then use your imagination to answer the questions.
- Revise the description so it provides complete, specific information about the employee's performance.

Original

> Although Jean has held the job of marketing assistant for nearly seven months, she still has trouble using the technology she needs to complete her job. Her attitude also leaves something to be desired. She does a great job in client meetings, though, and seems to enjoy that responsibility.

QUESTIONS	ANSWERS

REVISION

_____
_____
_____
_____
_____
_____
_____
_____
_____
_____
_____
_____
_____
_____
_____
_____
_____
_____

ANSWERS

Here are examples of questions and answers, as well as a suggested revision. Your responses will differ. But be sure your revision provides clear, specific information about the employee's performance.

Original

> Although Jean has held the job of marketing assistant for nearly seven months, she still has trouble using the technology she needs to complete her job. Her attitude also leaves something to be desired. She does a great job in client meetings, though, and seems to enjoy that responsibility.

QUESTIONS	ANSWERS
What kind of "trouble" does Jean have using technology?	• At least three times a week she asks for help with the online creative review program
	• Keith saw her — on four occasions during the last month — faxing changes instead of using the approved online program
What is meant by "her attitude leaves something to be desired"?	• She rolls her eyes and sighs loudly when corrected or when coworkers make suggestions to her
	• She interrupts others at least twice during most weekly staff meetings
	• She has complained to manager in the presence of other team members that most of the work she is being asked to do is "administrative" and "not what she signed on to do"
How was this information obtained?	• Observation
	• Staff comments
How long have these problems been going on?	• Six months, with the first month expected to be a learning period

QUESTIONS	ANSWERS
Does Jean have the skills and resources she needs?	• She was trained intensively during the first month, then registered for an online creative review program and client communication-processes training session
	• When she was hired, she was given a recently updated job description for marketing assistants that lists all the position's duties
Does Jean know what is expected? Has she been reminded?	• She has received written and verbal instructions and training
	• She has been retrained on the creative review system once and reminded about client communication processes at least twice
In what ways does she "do a great job in client meetings"? What does "seems to enjoy that responsibility" mean?	• She shows a clear understanding of clients' goals by paraphrasing them before presenting her ideas for solutions
	• She supports each of her ideas with clearly stated consumer research
	• She states that she enjoys client meetings and arrives at work early on meeting days to ensure that meeting materials are error-free and that they follow client communication processes

REVISION

Although Jean has held the job of marketing assistant for nearly seven months, coworkers say that she still asks for help at least three times a week when using the online creative review system. She has also been seen on four occasions in the past month faxing changes to clients, rather than using the approved online program as outlined in the client communication processes.

Jean was trained intensively during her first month in this job and then checked on her use of the online creative review technology and client communication procedures. Since then, she has received additional written and verbal instructions and training—for example, she was retrained on the creative review system at least once and reminded about correct client communication processes at least twice.

Jean does not seem to respond well to criticism or to coworkers' ideas and suggestions. When her performance is corrected or alternative ideas are suggested, she rolls her eyes and sighs loudly. During weekly staff meetings when ideas that differ from hers are suggested, she interrupts others before they are able to fully explain their suggestions. This occurs at least twice during most meetings. On two occasions after being corrected, she complained that the work she was being asked to do was administrative and not her job, despite the fact that the tasks she is being asked to complete are clearly outlined in the job description provided to her when she was hired.

One area where Jean excels in her job is in client meetings. She shows a clear understanding of the client's goals by paraphrasing them before presenting her ideas for solutions. She also supports each of her ideas with clearly stated consumer research. She has stated on multiple occasions that she enjoys client meetings and arrives at work early on meeting days to ensure that meeting materials are error-free and that they follow client communication processes.

On Your Own

Part 1

Read through the performance description you wrote at the end of Lesson 4.

- In the space below, list any questions that still need answering. As a guide, use the questions listed on pages 71 and 72, which are repeated here.

- Answer the questions.

- Revise the description as needed to be sure it's objective, complete, and specific.

> **QUESTIONS TO ASK**
>
> - How long?
> - How many?
> - Where?
> - How often?
> - When?
> - Who?

QUESTIONS	ANSWERS

REVISION

Part 2

Read through another sample of performance documentation you wrote (or read through Sample #1, #2, or #3 from the back of this book).

Follow the steps you learned in Lessons 4 and 5 to revise any part of that documentation that's unsupported opinion, vague, and/or incomplete.

REVISION

_____

_____

_____

_____

_____

_____

_____

_____

_____

_____

_____

_____

_____

_____

_____

_____

_____

_____

_____

_____

You've finished Lesson 5.

NOTES

NOTES

PROGRAM REVIEW

PART 1

If you're not sure how to answer any of the questions below, review each page that appears in parentheses after the question.

1. A performance objective (or performance standard) describes the following: (p. 9)

   _____

   _____

   _____

   _____

2. To be useful, most performance objectives should meet these criteria: (p. 10)

   _____

   _____

   _____

   _____

3. List three reasons why performance documentation must be clear, accurate, and free from bias: (p. 3)

   _____

   _____

   _____

4. Acceptable performance documentation includes enough information and uses specific, objective language to do the following: (p. 35)

   _____

   _____

   _____

5. Evaluations should not be based on the following: (p. 45)

_____

_____

_____

6. Subjective words can cause serious problems with performance documentation for these reasons: (p. 46)

_____

_____

7. Objective language describes the following: (p. 49)

_____

_____

_____

_____

_____

8. An evaluation is an opinion or conclusion that is based on the following: (p. 57)

_____

_____

_____

9. A description tells readers about the following: (p. 59)

_____

_____

_____

_____

_____

10. A description should include details that answer these six questions: (p. 71)

_____

_____

_____

_____

_____

_____

**Turn the page to check your answers.
Then continue to Part 2 of the Review.**

ANSWERS TO REVIEW PART 1

1. A performance objective (or performance standard) describes

   - what an employee will do to meet specific job requirements

2. To be useful, most performance objectives should meet the SMART criteria:

   - Specific — Are they specific?

   - Measurable — Are they measurable?

   - Achievable — Are they achievable?

   - Realistic — Are they realistic given the resources available?

   - Time — Are they time-bound?

3. List three reasons why performance documentation must be clear, accurate and free from bias:

   - A clear written record of discussions about performance issues can prevent misunderstandings

   - Clear documentation provides proof that employment decisions and actions were based on fair, objective, job-related criteria

   - What you write about a person's performance can become a record in a legal proceeding if a performance decision is challenged in court

4. Acceptable performance documentation includes enough information and uses specific, objective language to

   - describe behavior, performance, and results the evaluator has observed

   - explain, illustrate and support the evaluator's conclusions

   - tell employees clearly what they are doing well and what they need to improve

5. Evaluations must have a sound basis:

   - they must be observations of job-related behavior

   - they should not be impressions, assumptions, or opinions

6. Subjective words can cause serious problems with performance documentation because

   - they are open to so many interpretations

7. Objective language describes

   - observations

8. An evaluation is an opinion or conclusion that is based on

   - fact

9. A description tells readers about

   - what you observed (saw, heard, smelled, etc.) that led to your conclusion
   - the behavior you observed
   - what the employee said
   - what others say
   - results of work performed

10. A description should include details that answer these six questions:

    - How long?
    - How many?
    - Where?
    - How often?
    - When?
    - Who?

Turn the page for Part 2 of the Review.

PART 2

Circle the letter of the correct answer or answer questions on the lines provided.

1. Which of these performance objectives best meets the criteria for a useful objective?

    a. Create and manage a database so people can find a file under the name of the contact, the name of the sales representative, or the name of the company.

    b. Create files so people can find things.

2. What questions need to be answered to expand this general expectation into a useful performance objective?

    Pay more attention to data fields.

    _____

    _____

    _____

    _____

    _____

    _____

    _____

3. Which statement best meets the criteria for acceptable documentation?

    a. Susan gets confused too easily.

    b. Susan spent two days last week looking for the Berash file that she had misplaced.

4. Which of these statements conveys an observation?

    a. Instead of the two breaks allowed each day, Tim takes three or four.

    b. Tim takes too many coffee breaks.

5. Which statement is a description rather than an opinion or assumption?

    a. Melinda is never ready to work when she gets here.

    b. When Melinda arrives at work, she spends at least 15 minutes putting on her makeup and doing other personal tasks before she sits down at her desk.

6. Which statement is specific and complete?

    a. Royce doesn't like to plan his sales route, so he tends to zigzag across the county.

    b. Three times last month, Royce missed the delivery window for a customer. When I suggested he plan his sales route in advance, he said he doesn't need to plan.

7. List three questions you would ask if the following statement appeared in a performance document:

Patti's bad temper interferes with her ability to close sales.

_____

_____

_____

Turn the page to check your answers.

ANSWERS TO REVIEW PART 2

1. Which of these performance objectives best meets the criteria for a useful objective?

    (a.) Create and manage a database so people can find a file under the name of the contact, the name of the sales representative, or the name of the company.

    b. Create files so people can find things.

2. What questions need to be answered to expand this general expectation into a useful performance objective?

    Pay more attention to data fields.

    The questions you listed might include these:

    - What is the person doing wrong now?
    - What errors to the report format have been observed?
    - What changes need to be made?
    - What results will you observe when the report formats are acceptable?
    - What is the standard for acceptable reports with which the person's performance will be compared?
    - What is the timetable? (By when must the performance improve?)

3. Which statement best meets the criteria for acceptable documentation?

    a. Susan gets confused too easily.

    (b.) Susan spent two days last week looking for the Berash file that she had misplaced.

4. Which of these statements conveys an observation?

    (a.) Instead of the two breaks allowed each day, Tim takes three or four.

    b. Tim takes too many breaks.

5. Which statement is a description rather than an opinion or assumption?

    a. Melinda is never ready to work when she gets here.

b. When Melinda arrives at work, she spends at least 15 minutes putting on her makeup and doing other personal tasks before she sits down at her desk.

6. Which statement is specific and complete?

    a. Royce doesn't like to plan his sales route, so he tends to zigzag across the county.

    b. Three times last month, Royce missed the delivery window for a customer. When I suggested he plan his sales route in advance, he said he doesn't need to plan.

7. List three questions you would ask if the following statement appeared in a performance document:

Patti's bad temper interferes with her ability to close sales.

The questions you listed might include these:

- What behavior has been observed that demonstrates Patti's temper?
- How do you know that behavior interferes with her ability to close sales?
- What percentage of sales (or what number of sales) does she fail to close because of that behavior?
- How often does that behavior interfere with sales closings?

Congratulations! You've finished this program.

Keep this book as a reference to make sure you always write complete, accurate, objective performance documentation.

SAMPLE DOCUMENTATION FOR PRACTICE

Following this page are three typical examples of performance documentation and one job description. If you do not have examples of your own performance-related writing, you can use these samples for practice.

SAMPLE #1

Background Information

Janice Jordan works in the Customer Service Department of an insurance company. She was hired two years ago as a Representative I. Six months ago she was promoted to Representative II. Below is her first Progress Report since she started working in the new position.

PROGRESS REPORT: Janice Jordan

Janice is always courteous to her coworkers and supervisors. Her attitude toward extra work is always enthusiastic. She has good rapport with customers.

Since Janice began her new job, we have seen her blossom into a very warm and sociable Representative.

Janice is usually a strong contributor in weekly staff meetings. Occasionally Janice makes jokes in the meetings that others find inappropriate and disruptive.

Janice has been a big part of the team since Marge and Jerry left. Her skill and technical knowledge make her capable of handling most of the difficult situations that occur. Janice is a very valued asset to the office.

Janice can grasp new instructions with ease and needs little supervision with the tasks that have been currently assigned to her. Janice will seek assistance when faced with a new procedure.

Janice has superb attention to detail and excellent follow-through on her work. She never leaves her work for someone else to complete.

Janice is always at her desk on time and comes to work every day.

SUMMARY

Janice has been an asset to the smooth running of the office since the beginning of the year. In the time she has been here, she has been able to grasp her responsibilities with ease. She is bright and intelligent and has been a joy to work with, especially on stressful days. She is good with customers and with other staff, and she is very responsible.

SAMPLE #2

Background Information

Glenn Burkhart investigates insurance claims. An important part of his job is to prepare written reports that provide detailed information about his findings and conclusions.

Although his investigations are thorough and he keeps detailed notes, Glenn's reports are often sloppy, incomplete, and late. He has been told that his reports must meet specific guidelines and must be handed in on time. He has also been offered training to improve his report-writing skills. He has shown little progress since his last evaluation six months ago.

MEMO: Glenn Burkhart

Mr. Burkhart's reports are not acceptable. He does not seem to grasp (or does not care about) their importance. The reports are seldom written in an acceptable format, and they are often incomplete and sloppy. He also leaves out pertinent information. Many of his reports, furthermore, are late, and when he does turn them in I often have to ask him to do them over. This is a particular problem when Mr. Burkhart is given a rush assignment, to which he often reacts very negatively by complaining and becoming angry with other people in the office.

Mr. Burkhart's investigations are not the problem. He keeps very detailed notes and can clearly explain the reasons for his recommendations when we sit down and talk about them.

Mr. Burkhart and I have discussed this problem and he has agreed to improve his performance during the next three months by submitting most of his reports on time and making sure they are in the right format. He will also be more willing to take on rush assignments.

Mr. Burkhart understands that if his performance in this area fails to improve, he might be subject to discipline.

SAMPLE # 3

Background Information

Sarah Rening is completing her first year as an editorial assistant in the publications department of a large corporation.

PERFORMANCE APPRAISAL: Sarah Rening

PERFORMANCE SUMMARY:

Sarah is an excellent employee whose work is generally above standard. She is very well organized and communicates clearly. Although she needs some improvement in a few minor areas, she is undoubtedly one of the more valuable members of our staff.

COMPUTER SKILLS

Meets all standards; has shown improvement in proofreading.

GOAL: To continue to be aware of the need to proofread documents more carefully.

FILING

Her filing skills are excellent. She helped set up a new filing system devoted to our new acquisitions.

RECORD KEEPING

Her payroll and performance records are all up to date. Her time sheets are not always collected, reviewed, and sent to Payroll promptly.

GOAL: To get her time sheets to Payroll on time.

COMMUNICATIONS

She is an excellent communicator with printers, advertising reps, vendors, and graphic design staff. She sometimes lacks patience when discussing articles with authors.

GOAL: To be more tactful when she talks with authors about changes to their articles.

SAMPLE #3, PAGE 2

ONGOING PROJECTS

She compiled a very valuable Style Guide—a project she initiated. She has been assigned the job of developing author guidelines but has not gotten around to doing it.

GOAL: To develop author guidelines in a timely fashion.

ORGANIZING

Her excellent organizational skills are evident daily. She keeps her desk neat. She prepares and updates the publication schedule monthly and tracks publication status daily.

SAMPLE #4

Background Information

Julian Wong is an administrative assistant in a public agency. He is new to the job. His performance plan is to be based on the job requirements.

JOB DESCRIPTION   ADMINISTRATIVE ASSISTANT

CREATE DOCUMENTS

Produce neat, complete, accurate documents in a timely manner.

Follow District formats or special formats as instructed.

Proof typed documents for completeness and correct grammar, spelling, and punctuation.

MAINTAIN FILES

File memos, letters, and other documents as needed.

Keep files up to date.

KEEP RECORDS AND PREPARE REPORTS

Prepare monthly reports tallying employee expense reimbursement forms, purchase requisitions, and submit them to the Manager.

Log usage of Division vehicles.

PROCESS MAIL

Log, sort, and route incoming mail.

Log and route outgoing mail.

ORDER AND MAINTAIN SUPPLIES

Accept and review purchase requisitions, obtain Manager's signature when necessary, and send requisitions to Purchasing.

Inventory office supplies and order new supplies as needed.

Maintain the supplies closet.

SAMPLE #4, PAGE 2

PREPARE AGENDAS AND MEETING MINUTES

Prepare and disseminate the agenda for bimonthly staff meetings and other meetings as needed.

Take minutes when instructed and distribute them to meeting participants.

ANSWER TELEPHONES

Answer phones and route calls.

When needed, take messages.

MAINTAIN LIBRARY

Keep list of all books, magazines, articles, etc. that are available for staff members to check out.

Order new publications as requested and place them in the library when they arrive.

Maintain publication checkout log.

FOCUS ON YOUR DEVELOPMENT

Reviewing your own performance documentation can help you to become a better manager and a more effective and successful employee. Using the lessons that you have learned from this book, review performance documentation that has been written about you.

FROM LESSON 1: Review recent performance documentation that was written about you.

Does it contain enough information using specific, objective language for you to understand your strengths and opportunities?

Circle any statements that you do not fully understand. Create questions that you can ask the writer of the document.

FROM LESSON 2: Review recent performance documentation that was written about you.

Did the writer use observations to support subjective statements? Circle any subjective statements that you find. Underline any observations that support those statements. Are there any subjective statements that do not have supporting observations? Carefully observe your own performance. Are there examples or observations that would support the subjective statements? Consider what you would ask the writer, in light of these observations.

FROM LESSON 3: Review recent performance documentation that was written about you and contains evaluations and decisions.

Did the writer provide enough description for you to understand your strengths and opportunities? Did the writer present a description of the standard against which the result, behavior, or new skill would be measured?

FROM LESSON 4: Review recent performance documentation that was written about you that contains evaluations and decisions.

Are the descriptions specific and complete? Is there any language that you find vague? Are there questions that you could ask the writer that would help you capitalize on your strengths? Are there questions you could ask the writer that would help you identify and improve on your opportunities?

FROM LESSON 5: Review your current performance objectives.

Do the objectives clearly define expectations and standards for successful completion? Do the objectives describe performance that can be observed, measured, or both? Do they contain enough detail to be useful performance objectives for you and your team?

ACTION PLANNING

List three actions that you'll take to improve your performance documentation. Include a time frame.

LEARNING MORE ABOUT COMMUNICATING IN WRITING

Learning to write clearly doesn't stop with one book, one workshop, or one class. Learning to write is a lifelong pursuit, and you can always get better at it. Here are some ways you can continue to improve your writing skills:

USE WHAT YOU'VE LEARNED. People often spend time and money on books and courses and then ignore everything they've learned. Consciously and consistently use what you've learned in this book, and you'll find that all your written communications will continue to improve. You'll achieve the results you want and present a professional image of you and your organization.

KEEP LEARNING. Every writing book you read and every writing class you take will help you refine your skills. Take some business-writing workshops or classes; if your organization doesn't offer writing skills training, you'll find useful courses at your local community college or university extension. There are also some excellent self-study courses, both online and in workbook format.

ASSESS YOUR WRITING. Schedule time every few weeks to reread some of your recent e-mails and other documents you've written. It can be helpful to read your writing aloud to get a sense of the tone and see whether the sentences and paragraphs flow smoothly. Look at what you've written from the reader's point of view—making sure you've used the right tone, gotten the main point across clearly, answered all the reader's questions, organized the information logically, and presented the information so it's easy to read.

BE OBSERVANT. You can learn a lot from paying attention to other people's writing. When you read something that seems very easy to understand, ask yourself what the writer did that made the writing work. When you read something that's very difficult to follow, ask yourself what the writer should have done differently.

GET FEEDBACK. Other people often see things that we miss. Find a colleague whose judgment you trust, and periodically ask that person to give you specific feedback on your writing.

RESOURCES CONSULTED AND RECOMMENDED FOR CONTINUED LEARNING

Armstrong, Michael. *Performance Management: Key Strategies and Practical Guidelines,* 3rd edition. Kogan Page, 2006.

Armstrong, Sharon, and Madelyn Appelbaum. *Stress-free Performance Appraisals: Turn Your Most Painful Management Duty into a Powerful Motivational Tool.* Career Press, 2003.

Arthur, Diane. *The First-Time Manager's Guide to Performance Appraisals.* AMACOM, 2008.

Bruce, Anne. *Perfect Phrases for Documenting Employee Performance Problems.* McGraw-Hill, 2005.

Cokins, Gary. *Performance Management: Finding the Missing Pieces (To Close the Intelligence Gap).* John Wiley & Sons, 2004.

DelPo, Amy. *Performance Appraisal Handbook: Legal and Practical Rules for Managers,* 2nd edition. Nolo, 2007.

Falcone, Paul, and Randi Sachs. *Productive Performance Appraisals,* 2nd edition. AMACOM, 2007.

Grote, Dick. *The Performance Appraisal Question & Answer Book: A Survival Guide for Managers.* AMACOM, 2002.

Kirkpatrick, Donald L. *Improving Employee Performance Through Appraisal and Coaching,* 2nd edition. AMACOM, 2005.

Rudman, Richard. *Performance Planning and Review: Making Employee Appraisals Work,* 2nd edition. Allen & Unwin, 2003.

Weiss, Donald H. *Fair, Square & Legal: A Manager's Guide to Safe Hiring, Managing & Firing Practices,* 2nd edition. AMACOM, 2004.

NOTES PAGE 1

NOTES PAGE 2

NOTES PAGE 3

NOTES PAGE 4

NOTES PAGE 5

ABOUT WRITE IT WELL

Write It Well began business in 1979 as Advanced Communication Designs, Inc., a training company that specialized in helping people communicate clearly and work together effectively.

Our focus has always been on providing practical information, techniques, and strategies that people can use immediately. Our books and training programs are used by individuals, teams, training specialists, and instructors in corporations and businesses of all sizes, nonprofit organizations, government agencies, and colleges and universities.

The Write It Well series includes the e-learning module *Just Commas* and the self-paced training workbooks *Professional Writing Skills, Essential Grammar,* and *E-Mail: A Write It Well Guide.* For more about our company and detailed descriptions of our publications, visit our website, www. writeitwell.com.

ABOUT THE AUTHOR

Natasha Terk is the president of Write It Well and leads the firm's business operations and strategy. Natasha is the author of *Professional Writing Skills: A Write It Well Guide*, coauthor of *The Due Diligence Tool*, and contributing editor of *E-Mail: A Write It Well Guide.*

A recognized expert on business communication in the workplace, Natasha leads workshops, webinars, and consulting engagements for clients that include IKEA, Hitachi Data Systems, Hewlett-Packard, Granite Construction, Check Point Software Technologies, and the Port of Oakland. She develops job-relevant, engaging training solutions that help people work more effectively and efficiently.

Natasha served as program officer at the Packard Foundation, served as a management consultant with La Piana Consulting, and taught business writing at UC Berkeley. Natasha holds master's degrees from the University of San Francisco and the University of Manchester, UK.

CPSIA information can be obtained
at www.ICGtesting.com
Printed in the USA
FSHW020848201219